THE GALE & POLDEN TRAINING SERIES

FIGHTING PATROL TACTICS

By

COLONEL G. A. WADE, M.C.

AUTHOR OF
" The Defence of Bloodford Village," etc.

This book should be read
in conjunction with

" FIGHTING PATROL TRAINING "
" THE FIGHTING PATROL "

The Naval & Military Press Ltd

Published by

The Naval & Military Press Ltd
Unit 5 Riverside, Brambleside
Bellbrook Industrial Estate
Uckfield, East Sussex
TN22 1QQ England

Tel: +44 (0)1825 749494

www.naval–military-press.com
www.nmarchive.com

SUMMARY

PREVIOUS DESCRIPTION. .

Movement—Protection—**Instinctive reaction** to surprise.
Do unexpected thing.
Underlying principles.

POINTS BEFORE STARTING.

Enemy dispositions—Leader's intention—boundaries—
friendly patrols—own posts—expected back—where
to return—password—check arms, etc.
Flashes and rattles
Creaking boots.

PARACHUTISTS.

Count them.
Canister.
Attack quickly.
Not much ammunition.
Must move.
Objective—marked characteristic.
Rendezvous.
Interception.
Hold fire.
Morale of parachutists.
Harbour or dock? (Plate 1).
Mopping-up wood (Plate 2).

THE ATTACK.

Patrol really a **team.**
Attack best **defence.**
Sudden emergency—instinctive reaction.
Drill (Plate 3).
Dash and **yell.**
Blood lust.

THE DEFENCE.

Partridges—No Flanks—No Rear—Look-out in **every
direction.**
Drill (Plates 4 and 5).
Triangle very strong—**All-round Defence—Stillness** essen-
tial.

NIGHT PATROLS.

Night sight—hearing.
Slow, steady pace.
Silence.
Keep to low ground—keep off skyline.
Knowledge of country—stars—compass.
Use of " Signposts."
Risk of losing touch—passing messages.
Each man must keep touch back and front.
Distinguishing patches.
Use of " Sounds off."
Patience.
" Are you one of those sublime b.fs.? "

OBJECT OF FIGHTING PATROL.

" Kill without being killed."

NATURE ON OUR SIDE.

Bright little eyes.
Eager to tell us—blackbirds—lapwings—jays—foxes—
    weasels—rabbits.
Why not read them and be warned?
Patrol going into ambush.
Tom-tit: " Look-out! Look-out! "
Rabbit: " Danger close! "
Peewit: " In my meadow."
Sheep: " They are standing still."
Rooks: " Take care, take care! "
Patrol passes stolidly on.
Death awaits them.

TREES.

Crackles.

EARTH.

Footprints.

LIE OF LAND—WHAT TO LOOK FOR.

Enemy spots—human movement—bird or animal move
    ment—suitable bounds—covered approaches—ambushes.
Map study useful.

3

OBSERVATION—DEDUCTION—ACTION.

Plate 6 : " The rabbits told him."
Plate 7 : Which is the safe way out?

INDOOR TRAINING.

Sand table.
Map reading.
Tactical problems.
Communications.

CONCLUSION.

A very ordinary plan pushed with dash and determination
is far better than a most wonderful plan executed slowly
and half-heartedly.

FIGHTING PATROL TACTICS

I

In my previous lecture I have described the Fighting Patrol, its composition and its duties. You know how it moves in a purposeful and deadly manner across the countryside, protected from surprise by a screen of scouts.

You remember the patrol's instinctive reaction to sudden attack, and you have in the interval been practising these things.

Some of the elementary points of tactics were mentioned, such as the patrol never returning by the route used in its outward journey, and the advisability of frequently doing the **unexpected thing.**

So now we will study the action of the fighting patrol under various exciting circumstances so as to bring out those underlying tactical principles, the observance of which will solve many problems and whose neglect has on occasions greatly swelled the heavenly hosts.

But before setting out let us attend to the

POINTS BEFORE STARTING

If possible all members of the patrol should be taken to a point of vantage and given an opportunity of studying the ground over which they are to operate.

All should know very clearly:—

    (1) What is known of enemy dispositions or intentions.

    (2) The commander's intention.

    (3) Position of our own posts.

    (4) When patrol will be expected back and where it will return to.

    (5) The password or recognition signal they are to use.

    (6) Whether other friendly troops likely to be encountered have been warned of the patrol.

    (7) The boundaries of the area to be patrolled and approximate route to be followed.

    (8) Where friendly patrols may be encountered and how they will be recognized.

Arms, ammunition, bombs, etc., should be checked and men inspected for detection of anything upon them liable to flash in the sunlight or moonlight and also for rattles or anything likely to creak or knock against things.

(A pair of boots which creak are embarrassing enough going into church, but they are a hell of a sight worse within earshot of a heavily armed enemy.)

We will now show how the fighting patrol deals with those birds of ill-omen, the parachutists.

II

PARACHUTISTS

Parachutists furnish a new and very interesting tactical problem. No detachment of troops could be better for dealing with them than the fighting patrol, and there are certain

Points to be Observed in tackling Parachutists

(1) If you see them come down, COUNT THEM carefully and note where they alight.

(2) Usually their ammunition and automatic weapons are dropped in a separate canister. Watch for this and if you see it coming down note the spot and let the sections converge on it, because that is where the enemy will congregate. If you are very close send a party to get there first and ambush the parachutists, who will naturally assemble at the canister.

(3) If you cannot get there first, attack as quickly as possible. Remember that parachutists take an appreciable time to recover after the descent and bump, and they are " easy meat " if tackled quickly.

(4) The chief characteristic of the parachutist is that he has terrific fire-power, BUT NOT MUCH AMMUNITION; consequently, if you corner one draw his fire in any way possible (holding out caps, coats, etc.), and watch for an opportunity to snipe him.

(5) The parachutist is under the tactical disadvantage that he cannot " stay put " when he comes down. He *must* be up and moving, and he will not move promiscuously; he will move with a *definite objective*, so the Patrol Leader is at a great advantage if he can discover the parachutist's objective.

Their *immediate* objective is, of course, the canister of L.M.Gs. and S.A.A., but after that what will they do?

(a) They may have been told a rendezvous where they will assemble into a formidable body.

(b) They may have orders to converge singly or in small groups on a nearby vulnerable point or important tactical feature.

Usually both (a) and (b) have some marked characteristic, such as a wood on a hill or a factory chimney, so that they are easily recognizable by the parachutists.

Now, if the Patrol Leader is in a commanding spot he may be able to see towards which direction the various isolated parachutists are converging, and that will give him the idea where to intercept them. If the patrol are then quickly moved there by a covered approach they can lie in wait, remembering not to open fire too soon and to keep ABSOLUTELY STILL.

As the Germans approach, aim should be taken but the trigger should not be pressed till they show signs of seeing the patrol or are so close that a miss is impossible.

Once the enemy is aware of your presence he should be attacked with the greatest determination and gusto. If this is done, he will not put up much resistance, because he has already been strained to breaking-point. The journey across with its hazards and continual dread of Spitfires and Hurricanes—the apprehensions of the drop—the terrific jolt when he hits the earth—the feelings of uncertainty and dread when setting out in a hostile country—are all factors which undermine morale no matter whether the Hun concerned is a Nazi mystic or an ordinary German doped to the eyebrows.

Unless you are *very* close, do not waste ammunition shooting at descending parachutists. If you do shoot at them, AIM WELL BELOW.

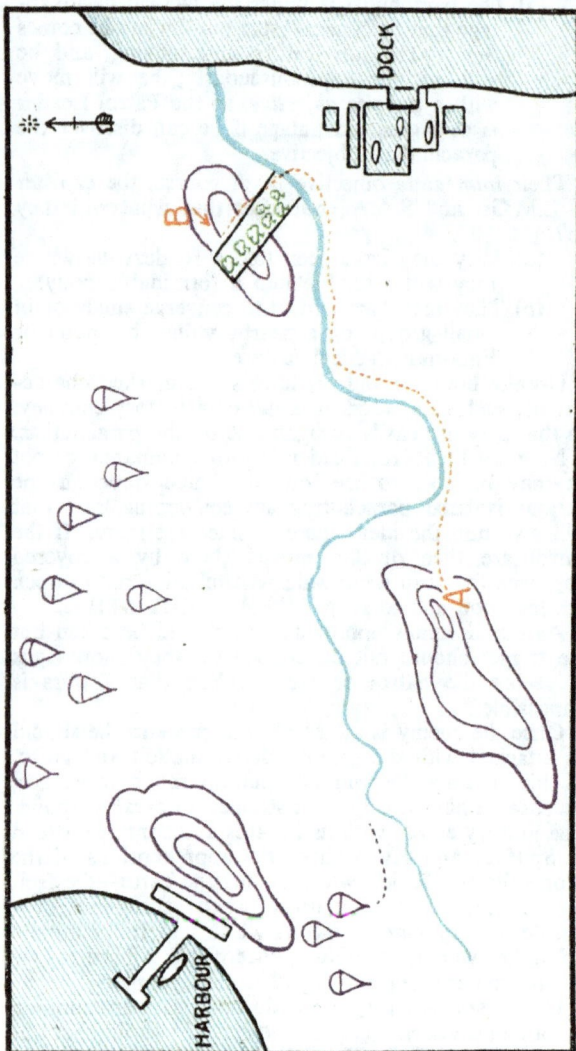

PLATE 1

DOCK

B

A

HARBOUR

8

This first plate illustrates just the sort of problem which will confront fighting patrols during an invasion, and you will see how the Leader, by a process of observation and reasoning, immediately evolves a plan for violent and successful action.

Attack on Parachutists

Patrol at A sees parachutists descend to the north and also a few to the west. Leader does not know which is their objective, the HARBOUR on the west or the DOCK on the east.

Watching the enemy on the north, he thinks he sees a movement towards the docks and when he sees that the parachutists which fell on the west are following the line of the stream he is convinced that the objective of the attack is the docks.

Where shall he intercept them?

He assumes that the Germans will assemble in the wood on the hill north-west of the docks and approach the docks that way.

ACTION.

He hurries the patrol along the bed of the stream and ambushes the enemy at B.

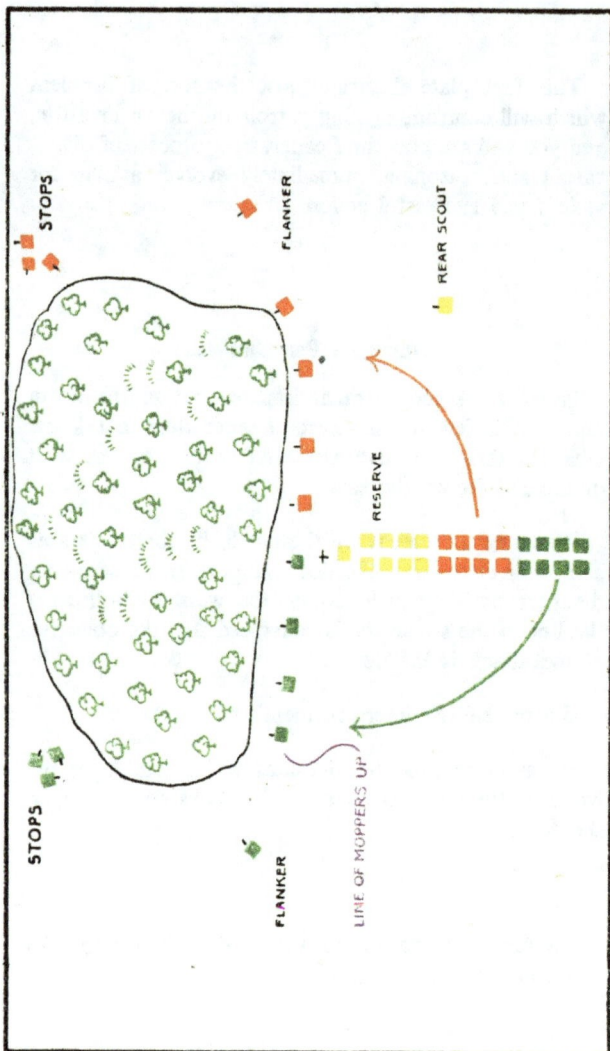

PLATE 2

Now we will consider a case in which parachutists have been reported in a wood or rough cover and the fighting patrol is after their blood (Plate 2).

The whole operation must be done quickly, systematically and without the least hesitation.

Mopping-up Parachutists, etc., in Wood or Rough Cover

If the area of the wood is greater than can be covered in one sweep, it should be divided into tasks to be taken one at a time.

The flankers and the reserve move forward at the same pace as the line of moppers-up. Flankers shoot enemy if he breaks cover on the sides, and the reserve can be immediately brought into operation should serious resistance be encountered.

Stops keep a watch on the far side of the wood and also a general look-out to guard against surprise from elsewhere when the patrol's attention is fixed on the wood. The stops can tell the position of the patrol in the wood by the position of the flankers.

Note the ever-present rear scout.

III

THE ATTACK

The fighting patrol is really a TEAM, and if it is to be successful it must be by virtue of dashing team work rather than by individuals performing daring deeds.

As a consequence, team tactics should be carefully studied and no opportunity lost of putting them into practice.

THE ATTACK represents 90 per cent. of the fighting patrol's duties, because the adage " Attack is the best defence " was never more fittingly illustrated than by the fighting patrol, which will nearly always defend itself by attacking its attackers.

Very often the fighting patrol will have little or no time in which to plan an attack upon the enemy, who may be met face to face suddenly and, possibly, unexpectedly.

The Germans may be just as surprised as the patrol. They should not be allowed a second to recover before the patrol is amongst them with butt or bayonet.

Even so, the attack should not be a blind, bloodthirsty rush, but should follow a definite plan put into execution by the patrol INSTINCTIVELY.

This instinctively correct action can be brought about only by making attack practice a DRILL.

This is illustrated in Plate 3.

Attack Drill

Patrol advances in column to within fifty yards of enemy (represented by red flag). On command " ATTACK," No. 1 Section deploys, lies down and opens fire instantly.

Nos. 2 and 3 Sections swing round to right and left respectively, break into line and charge on to the enemy's flanks, as shown.

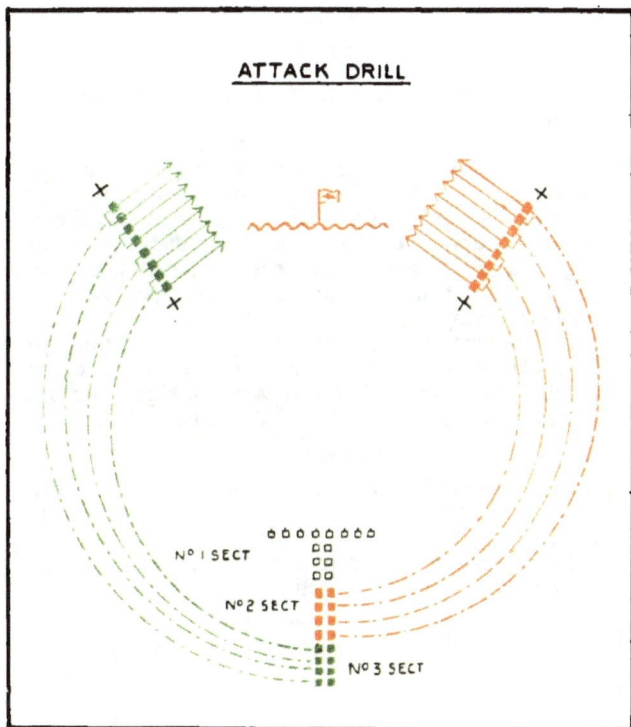

ATTACK DRILL

No 1 SECT

No 2 SECT

No 3 SECT

PLATE 3

When they reach X they should yell like fiends with the twofold object of scaring the enemy and letting No. 1 Section know when to cease fire, which is indicated in the drill by all No. 1 Section raising their muzzles.

In carrying out this drill, try to get the maximum DASH and the loudest possible YELL.

It is great fun and develops suitable bloodlust.

IV

DEFENCE

In addition to the attack drill there is a very interesting defence drill which everyone enjoys practising.

Have you ever seen a covey of partridges " jukking " for the night? The whole lot get together with their tails touching so that there is a beak pointing in every direction like points on a star. Over countless thousands of years partridges have found that this is the way to avoid disaster in darkness. No flanks, no rear and a look-out in every direction is their policy.

Make it yours!

If the patrol has to halt for any length of time the triangular formation should be taken up; each section jukking like a covey of partridges and taking advantage of any cover within forty or fifty yards.

Defence Drill

On command " DEFENCE! " No. 1 Section proceeds thirty yards and forms a small circle, men facing outwards.

No. 2 Section wheels to the right and forms circle forty yards from No. 1 Section.

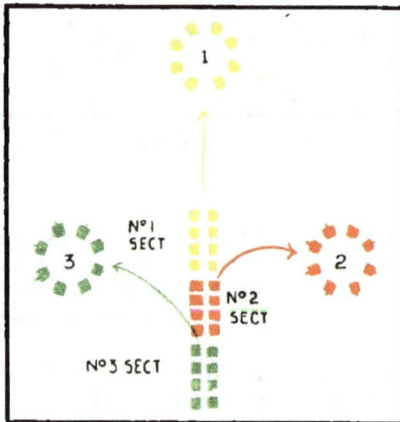

PLATE 4

No. 3 Section proceeds half-left and forms circle forty yards from Nos. 1 and 2 Sections.

Idea of forming the small circles is to rub in

All-round Defence

Practise slowly at first and then at the double. When men form circle they must keep ABSOLUTELY STILL, not even moving an eyelid, each section vying with the other to achieve statuesque immobility. The change from quick movement to rigidity is excellent training. Period of rigidity should be progressively increased.

Whenever the fighting patrol is halted, except between bounds, an endeavour should be made to assume this triangular formation. It is very strong and a good protection against surprise.

Scouts should be pushed out if there is dead ground anywhere near.

Advantage should be taken of any natural features to give protection or cover from view.

Once in position, the strictest discipline should be enforced to prevent MOVEMENT or NOISE.

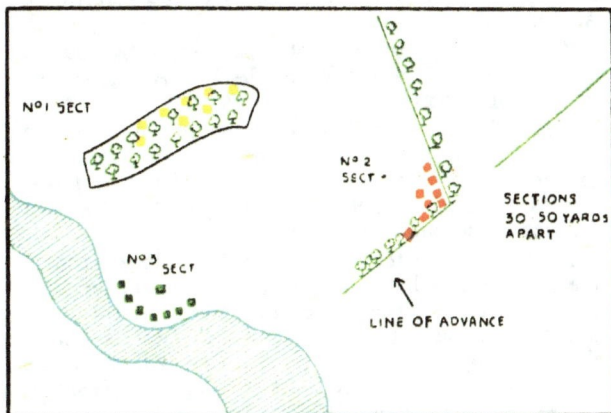

PLATE 5

V

NIGHT PATROLS

The Leader should know the "degree of NIGHT SIGHT" of each of his men.

This is easily ascertained by actual tests under blackout conditions. Men show a remarkable variation in ability to see at night and quite frequently men with excellent day sight prove nearly blind at night.

The best way of grading the men is to get them to count men, still and moving, at various distances in the dark.

Ability to see at night increases considerably with practice.

Hearing tests along similar lines should be devised so that the Patrol Leader knows EXACTLY the seeing and hearing capabilities of every man.

Quite frequently very good hearing is associated with poor night sight, and vice versa.

The advantage of the Patrol Leader having this information is that if two men are to be detailed to work together it can be arranged for two good ears to accompany two good eyes, which is the ideal arrangement and likely to do much for the efficiency of the patrol as a whole.

At night the patrol will not usually move by bounds, but will maintain a SLOW, STEADY PACE, pausing to listen frequently.

SILENCE is of the utmost importance from the moment of starting, and any member who habitually makes a noise, whether through clumsiness or talkativeness, should be put out of the patrol, as he is a menace to the safety of the rest.

By night, more than ever, it is desirable to keep to the LOW GROUND. The patrol can see better from there, and the chances of being seen when down in the hollows are much more remote. Also there is always the possibility that the low point of view will enable the patrol to catch the enemy silhouetted against the sky.

The low-lying ground is usually moister, softer and more suited to QUIET PROGRESS.

The skyline, even on quite a dark night, should be studiously avoided by the patrol. Light backgrounds may also be death-traps.

At night the patrol runs constant risk of losing two things—(a) DIRECTION and (b) TOUCH WITH ONE ANOTHER within the patrol.

Taking DIRECTION first, to maintain this the following are desirable:—

(1) Intimate knowledge of the country traversed, every tree, bush, hedge, fence and stream has certain features which, if carefully remembered, will tell you where you are.

(2) Practice in moving by luminous compass.

(3) A working knowledge of the stars.

(4) Familiarity with main features of the landscape from VARIOUS POINTS OF VIEW.

Sometimes the way can be indicated by " signposts " left by the patrol during daylight—pegs in the ground, piles of stones, wires, or blazing of trees.

It is frequently possible to get a good idea of the cardinal points by feeling the tree trunks. Often these slope away from the prevailing wind and have moss on the *leeward* side.

Now for the risk of LOSING TOUCH.

To counteract this calls for training and discipline. Usually the fighting patrol by night will consist of not more than seven men and the Leader, and they will normally advance in Indian file.

It is the imperative duty of each man to keep touch with both the man in front and the man behind him.

Should he lose touch with the man behind he should pass word forward *instantly* so that the patrol may halt and be re-formed.

White distinguishing patches on the back or, better still, on the seat of the trousers are a great help.

Patrols should learn to pass a message along the line by touching one another on the ankle or shoulder.

All men should frequently be practised in

(a) Location of sounds at night.

(b) Maintaining balance and feeling way in dark-ness.

(c) Falling quietly.

(d) Putting down HEELS first on SOFT ground.

(e) Putting down TOES first on HARD ground.

(f) Raising feet above long grass.

(g) Taking advantage of "sounds off" to cover their own noise.

With regard to (g), it is very seldom absolutely quiet at night, especially under war conditions, and if there is a nasty, crackly bit to be crossed, a little PATIENCE is all that is necessary. A pace when the distant gun fires (you know the sound is coming by the flash), another when the far-away train is shunting, and another when the gust of wind shakes the trees, gets the patrol across without detection.

But it takes PATIENCE. Have you got enough to do it that way?

Or are you one of those sublime b.fs. who would rather be shot than take a bit of trouble?

VI

OBSERVATION

At this point I would like to emphasize something which should be self-evident, but having seen so-called fighting patrols which seem in ignorance of it, I think it worth while, for everybody's sake, to rub it in. It is simply this: the object of all members of a fighting patrol should be to kill Germans **without being killed themselves.**

And there are various ways of avoiding sudden death at the enemy's hands, the principal one being to use your powers of observation. Nature is on our side against the invaders, and will tell us all sorts of things about them if we will only take heed.

Whenever a human being moves across the landscape his progress is watched by many bright little eyes far keener than ours. A hundred little nostrils give warn-ing of the intruder. Birds and beasts have their own way of reacting to human presence, and they are eager to tell us lots of things if we will try to understand their language.

The blackbird's twitter of alarm, the cry of the lapwing and its ungainly swoop, the scolding of the jays, the slinking away of the fox or the weasel, the sudden bolt of the rabbit or the thud! thud! thud! of its warning feet all have great significance in a countryside where an enemy is lurking.

Why not read them and be warned?

Time and again have I seen a patrol proceeding across country straight into an ambush regardless of the warnings being given by many friends, feathered and furry.

" There's someone behind those bushes. Look out! Look out! " whistled the tom-tit. " Danger too close for me—I'm off," said the rabbit. " They are walking right over my meadow," cried the peewit. " They are standing still now! " announced the sheep. " Somebody is hidden in our wood. Take care! Take care! " cawed the rooks.

And yet, disregarding all these warnings, the patrol passed stolidly on to where sudden death awaited them.

Trees can help you a lot. Beneath some the ground is grassy, moist and quiet. Underneath others are twigs which snap and crackle. Keep from under these, but note their position; some time you may hear a warning crack and you will then know exactly where to look (over your sights!).

Old Mother Earth will help you all she can; but you must read the expression on her face.

If you are in doubt as to the age of a footprint make one of your own close to it and compare the sharpness of the edges and the lie of the grass. The fresher the track the sharper the outline and the flatter the grass.

When studying the lie of the land prior to advancing across it the Patrol Leader should take note of:—

(1) Spots which the enemy may possibly be in occupation of.

(2) Any signs of human movement.

(3) Any bird or animal movement.

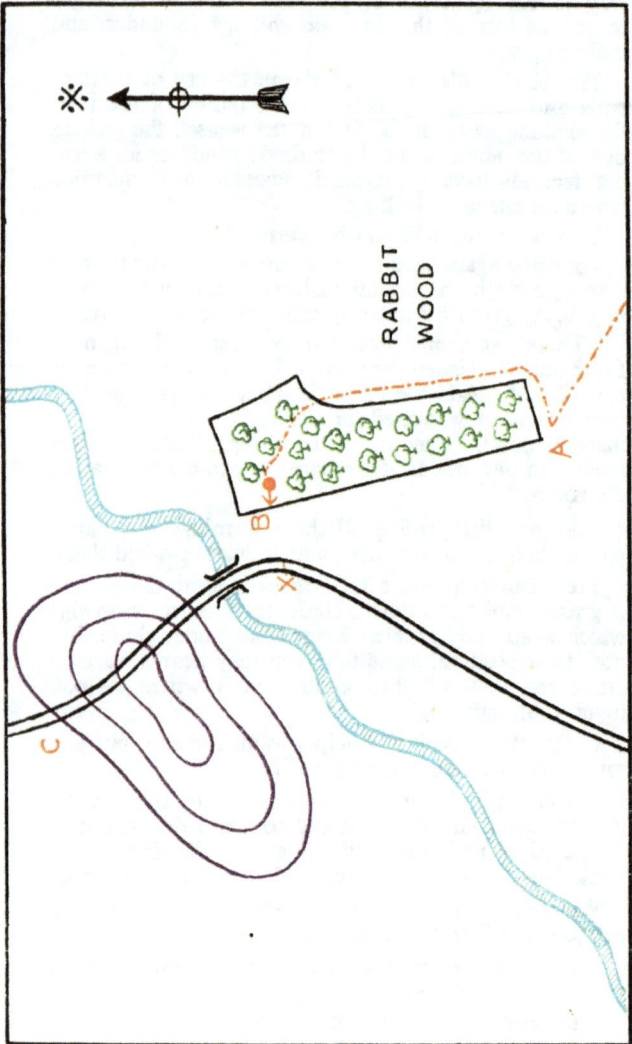

RABBIT WOOD

PLATE 6.

(4) Suitable places for bounds.

(5) Covered approaches to (4).

(6) Places likely to hide an ambush.

If possible he should carefully compare his observation with the map. In reaching quick decisions such as may be necessary in action, if the Leader (and every man, for that matter) has the MAP vividly impressed on his memory he has an immense advantage.

Here are two examples of how one Fighting Patrol Leader used his powers of observation and his brains to some effect: —

Observation, Deduction, Action !

Patrol Leader knows enemy is about and does not know if RABBIT WOOD is occupied. On arrival at A he sees rabbits feeding at B and assumes that there is no one in north end of wood. Suddenly he sees a rabbit sit up, sniff and lollop off into the wood, followed by the others. WHAT HAS ALARMED THEM? Nobody is in sight, therefore they have probably SCENTED an enemy. Which way is the wind blowing? From north-west. Someone is coming from the dead ground at C! Leader rushes patrol along edge of Rabbit Wood (he feels safe in doing this because the rabbits told him no one was inside), takes up an ambush at B, and scuppers the Germans at the bend in the road.

X marks the spot!

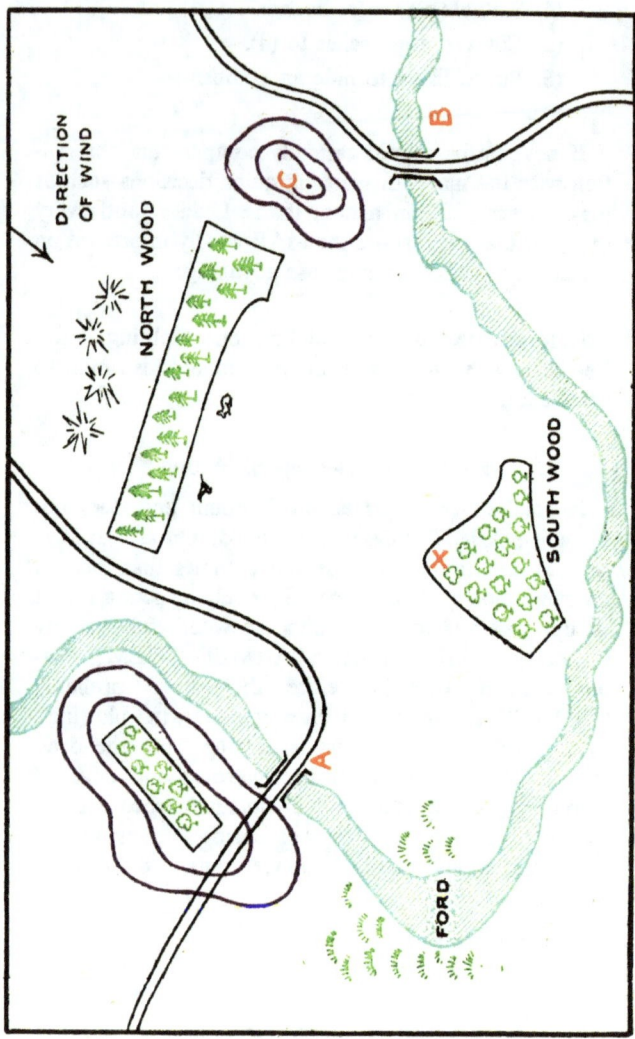

DIRECTION OF WIND

NORTH WOOD

SOUTH WOOD

FORD

A

B

C

PLATE 7

22

Observation, Deduction, Action !

Patrol has halted at X and hears sounds of shells far side of NORTH WOOD. Leader sees pheasants and rabbits run out of wood showing signs of distress. Concludes shelling was GAS. Wind is blowing straight towards patrol. He must get to a flank, but which way? He knows enemy is about, so which is the best route? River can be crossed by bridge A or B or the ford. Leader studies ground and sees rooks circling over wood north of A, so decides not that bridge. As he looks at the marsh by the ford several flights of ducks take off. Intruders there! Shall he try bridge B? He does not like it because patrol will be at mercy of any enemy on small hill C. Then he sees a large hawk circle round it and settle on a bare tree on the top. A shy bird! Nobody there! He knows he can pass bridge B safely if he goes quickly. That is the way to get out of a jam!

After giving the foregoing examples of fighting patrol tactics let me impress upon you all that, although much practice in the open air is required to make a really good patrol, there is a lot of very useful training which can be done INDOORS during winter evenings.

Schemes on the sand table, map reading, discussion on tactical problems, and practice in communications.

VII

CONCLUSION

The foregoing has been just a sketch outline of fighting patrol tactics.

It is an attempt to teach not so much what to do under all circumstances but how to develop a certain habit of mind; how to calmly contemplate exciting facts, and how to collect by keen observation evidence which will enable you to make a plan to outwit the enemy.

Remember.—There is nearly always time to make a PLAN (and where there is not your **instinctive drill movements** will take care of things), so make it as deliberately as you can, **but**, having made it, go all out for its successful execution with every ounce your patrol possesses.

A very ordinary plan pushed with dash and determination is far better than the most wonderful plan executed half-heartedly and slowly.